ZEUS

By Christine Ha

WWW.APEXEDITIONS.COM

Copyright © 2022 by Apex Editions, Mendota Heights, MN 55120. All rights reserved. No part of this book may be reproduced or utilized in any form or by any means without written permission from the publisher.

Apex is distributed by North Star Editions:
sales@northstareditions.com | 888-417-0195

Produced for Apex by Red Line Editorial.

Photographs ©: Shutterstock Images, cover, 1, 6, 7, 8–9, 10–11, 12–13, 14, 15, 16–17, 18–19, 20–21, 22–23, 24–25, 26, 27, 29; iStockphoto, 4–5

Library of Congress Control Number: 2020952925

ISBN
978-1-63738-017-8 (hardcover)
978-1-63738-053-6 (paperback)
978-1-63738-123-6 (ebook pdf)
978-1-63738-089-5 (hosted ebook)

Printed in the United States of America
Mankato, MN
082021

NOTE TO PARENTS AND EDUCATORS

Apex books are designed to build literacy skills in striving readers. Exciting, high-interest content attracts and holds readers' attention. The text is carefully leveled to allow students to achieve success quickly. Additional features, such as bolded glossary words for difficult terms, help build comprehension.

TABLE OF CONTENTS

CHAPTER 1
DEADLY LIGHTNING 5

CHAPTER 2
ZEUS THE MIGHTY 11

CHAPTER 3
RISE TO POWER 17

CHAPTER 4
WORSHIPPING ZEUS 23

Comprehension Questions • 28

Glossary • 30

To Learn More • 31

About the Author • 31

Index • 32

CHAPTER 1
DEADLY LIGHTNING

Zeus looked down from his throne on Mount Olympus. He saw an army of giants. They climbed up the mountain and began to attack.

Mount Olympus is the highest mountain in Greece. Legends say it was the home of the gods.

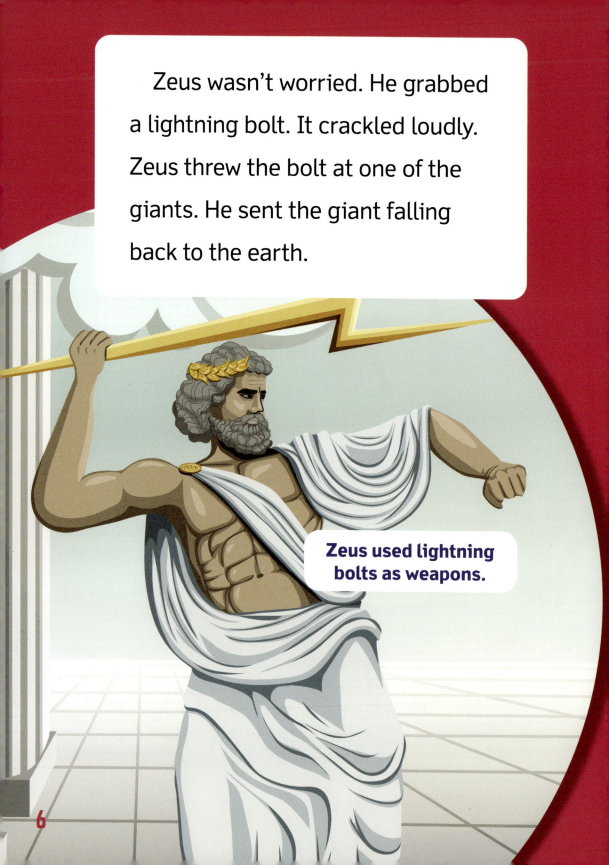

Zeus wasn't worried. He grabbed a lightning bolt. It crackled loudly. Zeus threw the bolt at one of the giants. He sent the giant falling back to the earth.

Zeus used lightning bolts as weapons.

In some stories, the goddess Nike drove Zeus's chariot for him.

WIND GODS

In addition to Zeus, the Greeks worshipped four wind gods. Some stories say these gods turned into horses to pull Zeus's **chariot**.

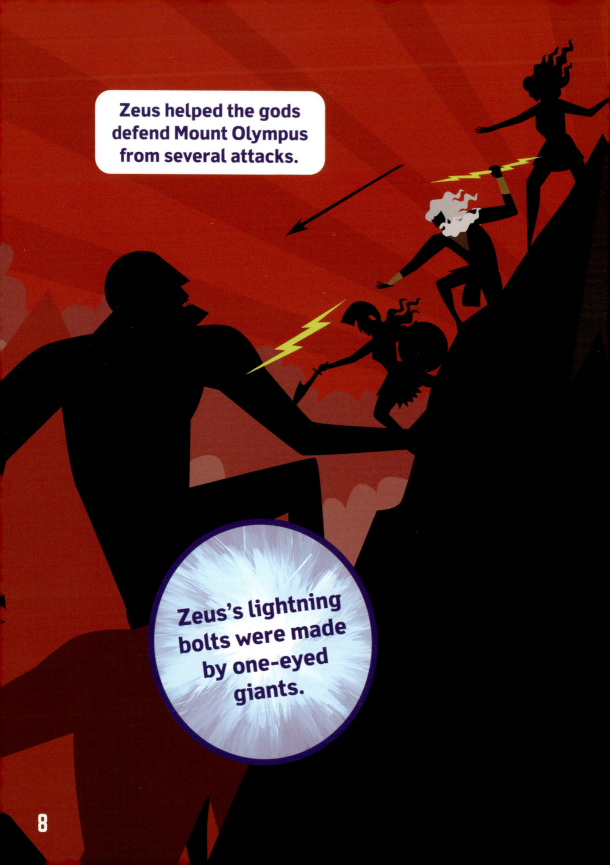

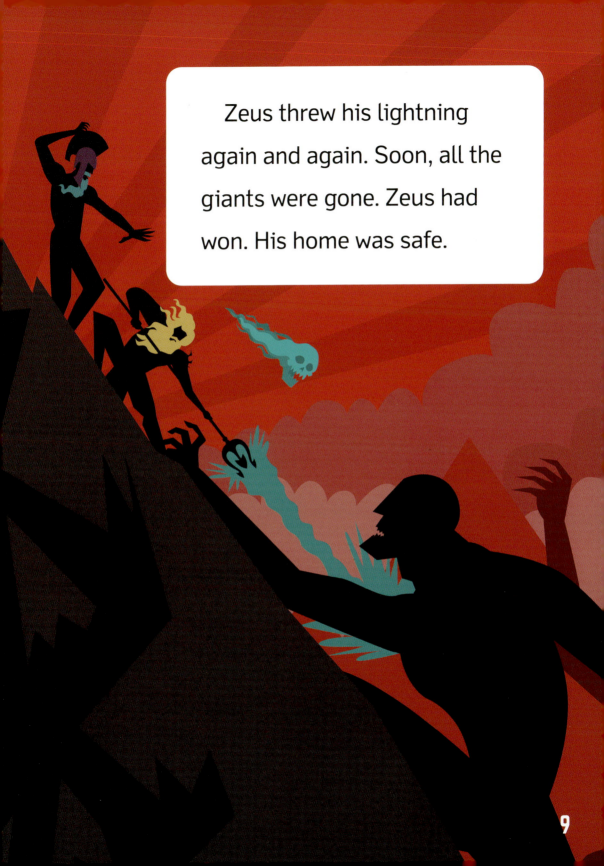

Zeus threw his lightning again and again. Soon, all the giants were gone. Zeus had won. His home was safe.

CHAPTER 2
ZEUS THE MIGHTY

Zeus was the god of thunder and lightning. He had power over weather. He could control storms, rain, and wind.

Zeus had a golden eagle. It carried messages for him.

Zeus ruled both gods and humans. He watched over them from Mount Olympus. Zeus **punished** evil people. But he rewarded good deeds.

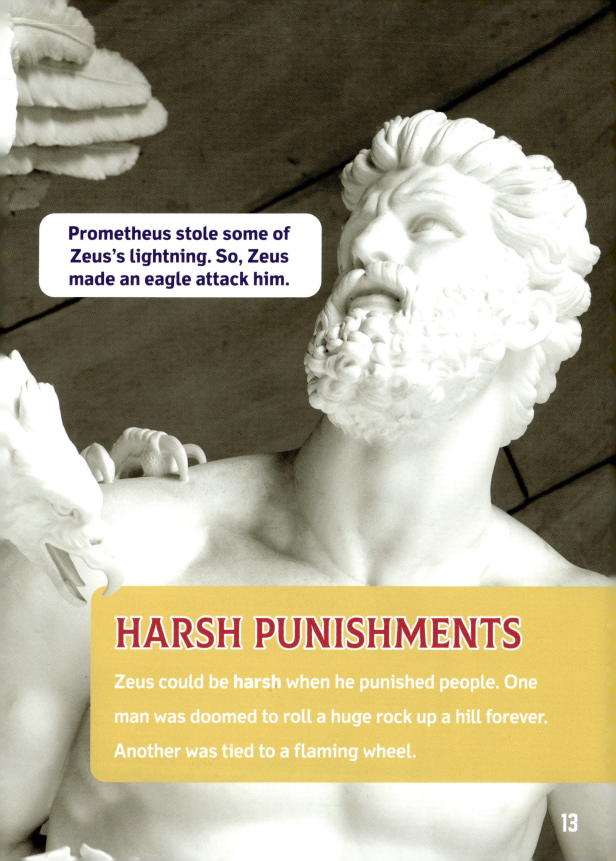

Prometheus stole some of Zeus's lightning. So, Zeus made an eagle attack him.

HARSH PUNISHMENTS

Zeus could be **harsh** when he punished people. One man was doomed to roll a huge rock up a hill forever. Another was tied to a flaming wheel.

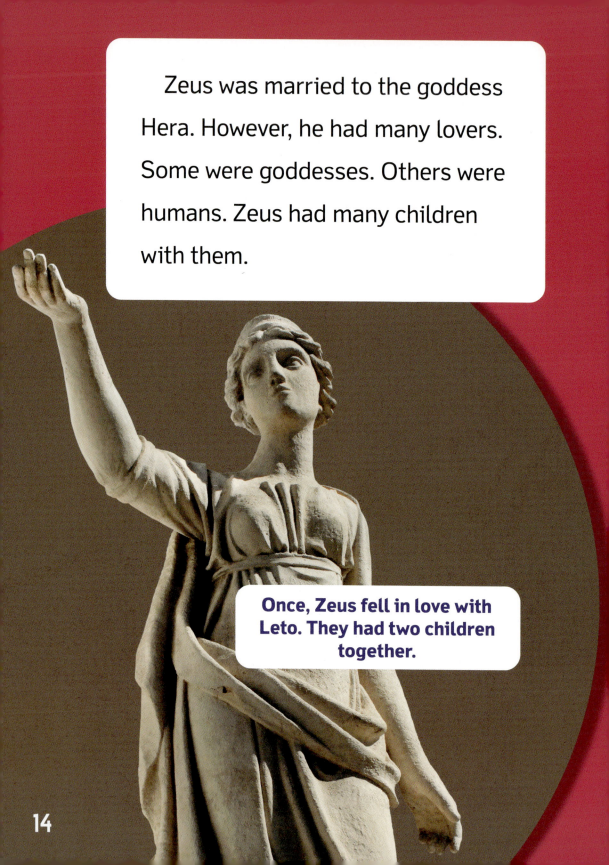

Zeus was married to the goddess Hera. However, he had many lovers. Some were goddesses. Others were humans. Zeus had many children with them.

Once, Zeus fell in love with Leto. They had two children together.

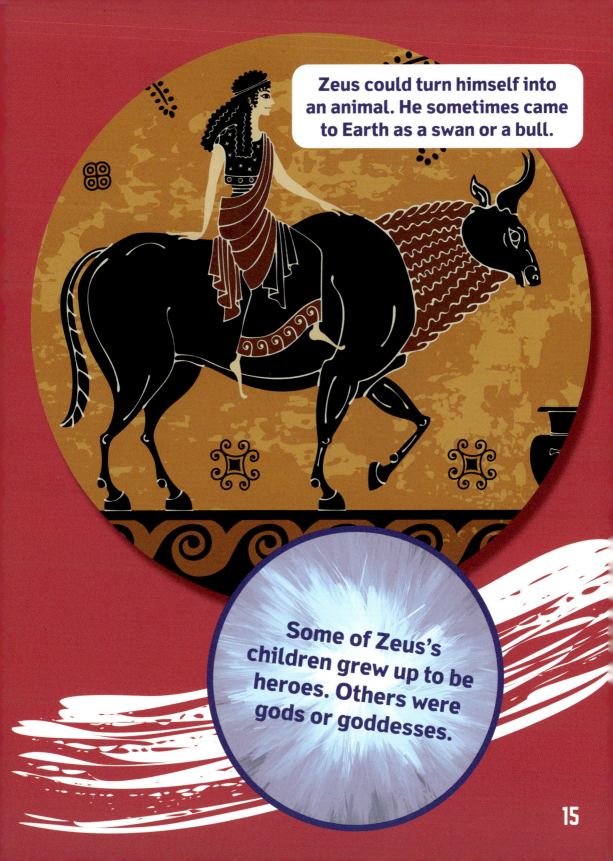

CHAPTER 3

RISE TO POWER

According to legend, Zeus was the son of Cronus. Cronus was a **Titan**. He ruled the world. But he was told his children would **overthrow** him.

Legends say Cronus ruled over harvests. Farmers prayed to him for help growing crops.

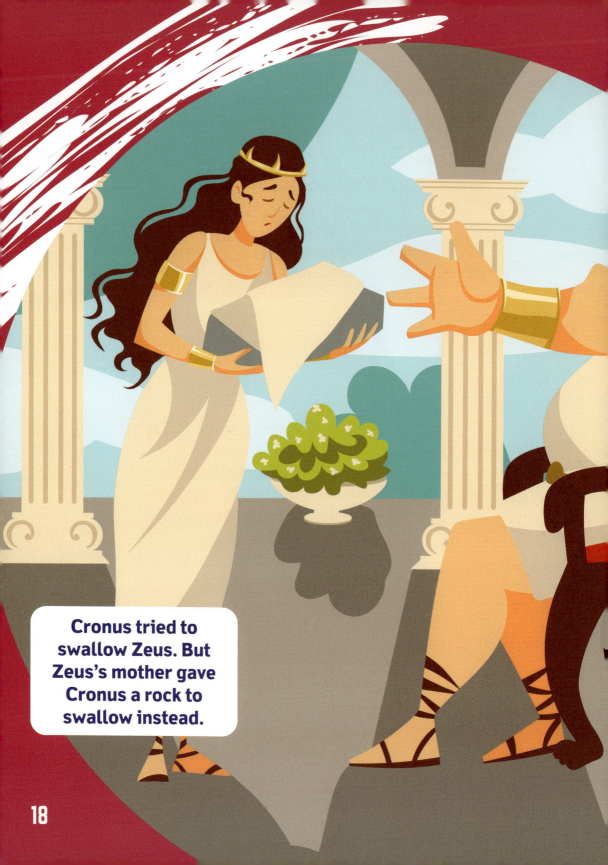

Cronus tried to swallow Zeus. But Zeus's mother gave Cronus a rock to swallow instead.

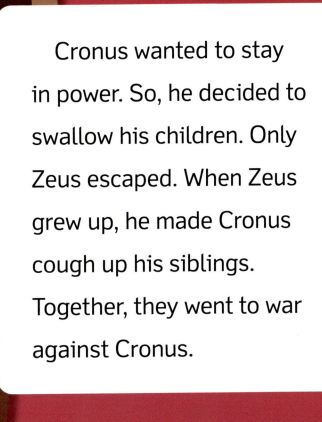

Cronus wanted to stay in power. So, he decided to swallow his children. Only Zeus escaped. When Zeus grew up, he made Cronus cough up his siblings. Together, they went to war against Cronus.

The gods Hades and Poseidon were Zeus's brothers.

The war lasted 10 years. Finally, Zeus took the throne from his father. He became the new ruler.

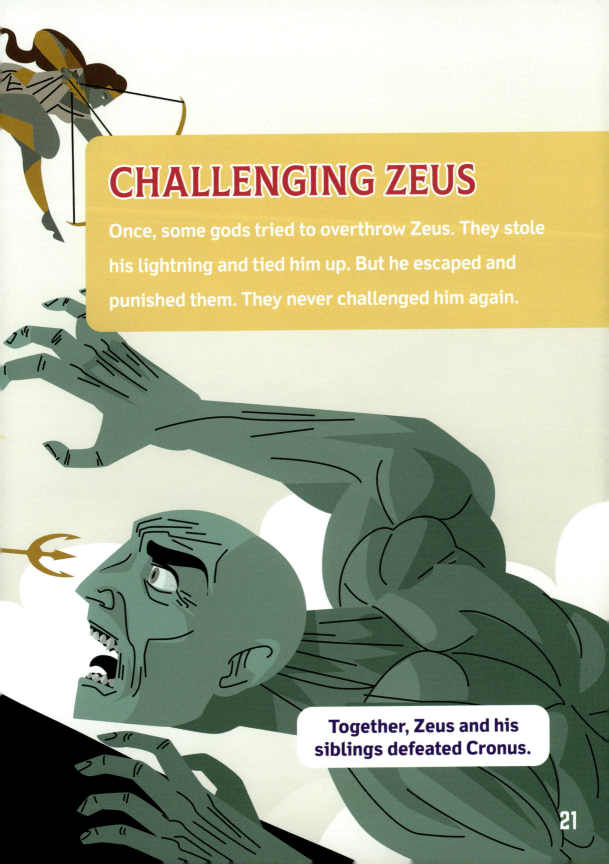

CHALLENGING ZEUS

Once, some gods tried to overthrow Zeus. They stole his lightning and tied him up. But he escaped and punished them. They never challenged him again.

Together, Zeus and his siblings defeated Cronus.

CHAPTER 4
WORSHIPPING ZEUS

Zeus was popular all over Greece. Many homes had an **altar** to him. People believed Zeus would protect their families.

Zeus is often shown as a strong man with a long beard.

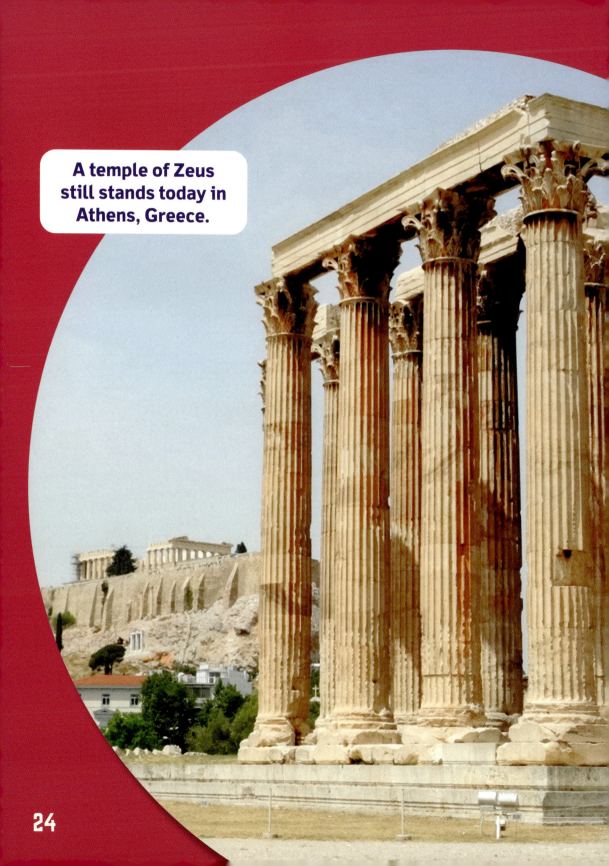

A temple of Zeus still stands today in Athens, Greece.

The Greeks also built temples for Zeus. The temples stood on hills or mountains. People visited them to pray for rain.

One temple had a huge statue of Zeus. It stood about 40 feet (12 m) tall.

One major temple was in Olympia. This city **hosted** the Olympic Games. This **festival** was held to honor Zeus. It featured many sports.

Discus throwing was part of the Olympics. A discus is a heavy metal plate.

Olive trees grew near Zeus's temple in Olympia. Their leaves were symbols of victory and peace.

At the Olympics, winners were given crowns of olive leaves.

OLYMPIC GAMES

The Olympic Games took place every four years. People came from all over Greece to watch and **compete**. Events included races and wrestling.

COMPREHENSION QUESTIONS

Write your answers on a separate piece of paper.

1. Write a few sentences explaining how Zeus came to power.

2. Do you think Zeus was a good ruler? Why or why not?

3. What kind of being was Cronus, Zeus's father?
    - **A.** a human
    - **B.** a hero
    - **C.** a Titan

4. Why might temples for Zeus be built on mountains?
    - **A.** The temples could be near the sky and weather.
    - **B.** The temples could be too high to visit.
    - **C.** Only people on mountains worshipped Zeus.

5. What does **rewarded** mean in this book?

*Zeus punished evil people. But he **rewarded** good deeds.*

    A. thanked people for doing things
    B. stopped people from doing things
    C. hurt or made fun of people

6. What does **popular** mean in this book?

*Zeus was **popular** all over Greece. Many homes had an altar to him.*

    A. not very well-known
    B. liked by many people
    C. very hard to find

Answer key on page 32.

GLOSSARY

altar
A table used for prayers, offerings, or other religious actions.

chariot
A two-wheeled cart pulled by horses or other animals.

compete
To try to beat others in a game or event.

festival
A day or time of celebration, often based on a religion.

harsh
Very hard or mean, especially in a way that is unfair.

hosted
Planned an event or provided the space where it happened.

overthrow
To remove someone from power.

punished
Forced someone to do something hard or painful after doing something wrong.

Titan
A type of huge, powerful giant. In Greek mythology, Titans ruled the earth before the gods did.

TO LEARN MORE

BOOKS

Flynn, Sarah Wassner. *Greek Mythology.* Washington, DC: National Geographic, 2018.

Menzies, Jean. *Greek Myths: Meet the Heroes, Gods, and Monsters of Ancient Greece.* New York: DK Publishing, 2020.

Temple, Teri. *Zeus: King of the Gods, God of Sky and Storms.* Mankato, MN: The Child's World, 2019.

ONLINE RESOURCES

Visit **www.apexeditions.com** to find links and resources related to this title.

ABOUT THE AUTHOR

Christine Ha lives in Minnesota. She enjoys reading and learning about myths and legends from around the world. She would love to watch the Olympics in person one day.

INDEX

A
altar, 23

C
chariot, 7
children, 14–15, 17, 19
Cronus, 17, 19

G
giants, 5–6, 8–9

H
Hades, 19

L
lightning, 6, 8–9, 11, 21
lovers, 14

M
Mount Olympus, 5, 12

O
Olympia, 26
Olympic Games, 26–27

P
Poseidon, 19
punishment, 12–13, 21

R
rain, 11, 25

T
temples, 25–26
throne, 5, 20
thunder, 11
Titan, 17

W
war, 19–20
weather, 11
wind, 7, 11

Answer Key:
1. Answers will vary; **2.** Answers will vary; **3.** C; **4.** A; **5.** A; **6.** B